T0354650

LOVE

MUST HAVE A

BODY

T. L. HARPER

WESTBOW
PRESS®
A DIVISION OF THOMAS NELSON
& ZONDERVAN

THE HOLY BIBLE, NEW INTERNATIONAL VERSION®, NIV® Copyright © 1973,
1978, 1984, 2011 by Biblica, Inc.® Used by permission. All rights reserved worldwide.

The Living Bible copyright © 1971 by Tyndale House Foundation. Used
by permission of Tyndale House Publishers Inc., Carol Stream, Illinois
60188. All rights reserved. The Living Bible, TLB, and the The Living
Bible logo are registered trademarks of Tyndale House Publishers.

Scripture taken from The Message. Copyright © 1993, 1994, 1995, 1996,
2000, 2001, 2002. Used by permission of NavPress Publishing Group.

The New Testament in Modern English by J.B Phillips copyright
© 1960, 1972 J. B. Phillips. Administered by The Archbishops'
Council of the Church of England. Used by Permission.

WestBow Press books may be ordered through booksellers or by contacting:

WestBow Press
A Division of Thomas Nelson & Zondervan
1663 Liberty Drive
Bloomington, IN 47403
www.westbowpress.com
1 (866) 928-1240

Because of the dynamic nature of the Internet, any web addresses or links contained in
this book may have changed since publication and may no longer be valid. The views
expressed in this work are solely those of the author and do not necessarily reflect the
views of the publisher, and the publisher hereby disclaims any responsibility for them.

Any people depicted in stock imagery provided by Thinkstock are models,
and such images are being used for illustrative purposes only.
Certain stock imagery © Thinkstock.

ISBN: 978-1-5127-9782-4 (sc)
ISBN: 978-1-5127-9783-1 (hc)
ISBN: 978-1-5127-9781-7 (e)

Library of Congress Control Number: 2017912014

Print information available on the last page.

WestBow Press rev. date: 10/17/2017

ABOUT THE AUTHOR

T. L. Harper is one of five siblings, with two adult children (Rohman and Alayna). He also has a diverse background that lends itself to the depth of thinking this work presents. T. L. Harper is well traveled internationally and has an eclectic list of accomplishments including dozens of published gospel songs for over 40 years, a Dove Award Song of the Year nomination, nationally distributed recordings and Degrees in Theology and Music. His life experiences makes him uniquely qualified to present material that fosters thought provoking meditation and contemplation of the world around us and our place in it. You, the Reader will enjoy the hidden insights T. L. Harper reveals within the story lines that follow.

ACKNOWLEDGEMENT

I want to thank all those friends and family for their support in the preparation of this work. All those who reviewed this work and gave their honest feedback and observations that have aided in this works final presentation.

ACKNOWLEDGMENT

DEDICATION

This Book is dedicated to the purpose of answering many of the questions that puzzle both believers and non-believers alike, as to How and Why God has chosen such unique methods of revealing Himself to humanity. My hope is, you will meditate on the answers each "question statement" reveals, and will walk away with a greater appreciation and awareness of just how creative *Elohim* is in the making of this inextricable universe we occupy, and the unique relationship, we as human *spirit-beings* have in that *Divine* order.

PREFACE

Although small in the number of pages, this is a work you will want to revisit time and time again. Why? Each time you read and meditate on what this book presents about the subject, its revelations will pull you into new statures of faith. You will discover new thresholds of awareness and assurance of God's Love, what Love is, and how that same Love is reflected in daily life.

We will explore 20 "Why" Statements in the Chapters that follow. Each Chapter holds a "story" within a "larger Story". This little book will be a continual reminder that we are here for a purpose. Each one of us occupies a place of significance and influence. And in that place of influence, are opportunities to experience *Faith, Hope* and *Love*; but the greatest of these is *Love*.[1]

---

[1] I Corinthians 13:13 (NIV)

INTRODUCTION

I n this book, I attempt to explore some of the ways in which *Elohim* {GOD} expressed himself. Some view the Bible as one big gigantic screen play, where all humanity are simply pawns and puppets moved here and there as the story-line is meant to unfold. We will discover it is much, much more than that.

We will discover that *Elohim* revealed himself by the most elaborate display of creativity imaginable. For it is written, *"He is before all things, and in Him all things hold together."* [2] The essence of who we are and why we are here reveals itself in our looking into the *divine* nature of God which contains both history *revealed* through prophets and apostles, and by the *Spirit of revelation* concerning the future. In this way, we glimpse the majesty of heaven in a way that is life changing for us in the here and now. The door is always open to *divine* experience. For it is written, *"God has revealed it to us by his Spirit. The Spirit searches all things, even the deep things of God."*[3]

There are others who believe that, if {GOD} is really out

---

[2] Colossians 1:18 (NIV)
[3] I Corinthians 2:10 (NIV)

there somewhere, He is beyond knowing. We will discover that God has taken special care and intention to make Himself known to humankind. He wants us to know Him. God wants us to know that HE knows each one of us by name. God wants us to know HIM in a way that is life-altering and life giving. The very God **Elohim** tells us, *"You will seek me and find me when you seek me with all your heart."*[4]

God delights in His creation, loves each one of us individually with a *perfect* love. Even if you don't believe in Him, He believes in you. And, if you don't think you can get to Him, HE can and will get to you. That's how much HE loves you. For it is written, *"Even when we are too weak to have any faith left, He remains faithful to us and will help us for He cannot disown us who are a part of Himself and He will always keep His promises to us."*[5]

---

[4] Jeremiah 29:13 (NIV)
[5] 2 Timothy 2:13 (Living Bible)

CHAPTER ONE

Why a Creator

Have you ever wondered how and why God exists? Or why He would make such a vast expanse of the universe? Why did He form the Earth and pay such meticulous attention to every detail of its design? Why did He make such diverse animal life? Why are there such intricacies of the human form? What did God have in mind? And why? It is written, *"When I look up into the night skies and see the work of your fingers, the moon and the stars you have made, I cannot understand how you can bother with mere puny man, to pay any attention to him!"* [6]

Science postulates that there are at least one hundred billion galaxies similar to ours. Each galaxy has an estimated one hundred billion stars. Science also suggests that our inexplicable and marvelous universe is still expanding and creating new galaxies. It is written, *"The heavens tell about the glory of God. The skies show that his hands created them. Day after day they speak about it. Night after night they make it known. But they don't speak or use words. No sound is heard from them. Yet their voice goes out into the whole earth. Their words go out from one end of the world to the other."* [7]

But why would *Elohim* do all this? We know our universe is a "created space" and that infinite space lies beyond its defined borders. Science theorizes that at least nine different dimensions exist, maybe more. We know for certain that we live in two different dimensions at the same time; a physical one, and a spiritual one. Both occupy the same time and space; and yet, much more lies beyond the imagination of our understanding.

---

[6] Psalms 8:3-4 (Living Bible)

[7] Psalms 19:1-4 (NIV Readers Version)

Modern science appears to disagree with the biblical record on how our universe began. However, science does agree with the Holy Scriptures on one basic principle of our universe's beginnings; *"what is seen was not made out of what was visible."* [8] Science admits that our universe, and all we see and know, began from an *invisible* source no one can see known as *invisible matter.* And from it science suggests the *"Big Bang"* theory. This theory postulates that all we see came from a sub-atomic particle half the size of an atom. The Big Bang, as science likes to refer to it, was really nothing more than the *Voice of Elohim* speaking something into existence that had never been there before. *"We understand that the universe was formed at God's command, so that what is seen was not made out of what was visible."* [9] The *"Big Bang"* occurred when God said, "LET THERE BE" and *BANG!* - "THERE IT WAS".

Our universe could not exist if the protons and neutrons that make up the Earth's physical structure were either bigger or smaller. They just *happened* to be EXACTLY the right size. Science has no explanation for this. Of course, we know it to be *divine* order. Science must admit the fact that, *"just because you can't see, it, doesn't mean it isn't there."* Just because no one saw *Elohim* create the universe, doesn't mean He didn't create it. Even Science admits some original *Intelligent* Source had to be involved in creating all this. For it is written, *"The Lord's*

---

[8] Hebrews 11:3 (NIV)

[9] Hebrews 11:3 (NIV)

wisdom founded the earth; his understanding established all the universe and space."[10]

Elohim exists because He made things from His own essence to be *visible* to show He exists. Without *creation*, we would know nothing of the nature and character of God. We know there is a God by the very things He has made. It is written, *"For since the creation of the world, God's invisible qualities; his eternal power and divine nature have been clearly seen, being understood from what has been made, so that men are without excuse."* [11] In another place it is written, *"He {**Elohim**} has not left himself without testimony; He has shown kindness by giving you rain from heaven and crops in their seasons; he provides you with plenty of food and fills your hearts with joy."* [12]

In the book of Job, the oldest book of the biblical record, the acknowledgment of God compels us to inquire of the many *witnesses* to creation. It is written, *"But ask the animals, and they will teach you, or the birds of the air, and they will tell you; or speak to the earth, and it will teach you, or let the fish of the sea inform you. Which of all these does not know that the hand of the LORD has done this? In his hand is the life of every creature and the breath of all mankind."* [13]

This then, raises yet another question. *Why a Creation?*

---

[10] Proverbs 3:19 (Living Bible)
[11] Romans 1:20 (NIV)
[12] Acts 14:16-17 (NIV)
[13] Job 12:8-10 (NIV)

CHAPTER TWO

Why a Creation

W hy would God need to create *anything* at all? He exists in perfect harmony without the need of anything outside Himself. Was it that **Elohim** wanted to express HIS presence by creating magnificent celestial wonders to show He exists? Or to show His magnificent creative ability beyond any imagination? Or was there more to His intent than this? When you're God, and can do anything you want, you don't have an ego, or need to prove anything to impress anybody.

As hard as Science tries to ignore this reality, there is no other plausible explanation of our universe' beginnings outside a *Divine enactment*. Without God, we are left with unanswerable questions: Where did *matter* come from? How did it get here to begin with? How did it come to form such an awesome, and elaborate universal design? Where and how did such diversity of life come into being from what would otherwise be called *sterile matter?*

Because it is "too wonderful" for humankind to contemplate the awesome existence and creativity of an omnipotent Creator, God challenges us to take Him at His Word, the same Word that created the universe. So we are left with the question; Do I believe the atheist's or agnostic's view that *all creation* just happened by itself, through some cosmic accidental occurrence? Or do we, as the Writer of Hebrews suggests, accept that "*without faith it is impossible to please God, because anyone who comes to Him must believe that he exists and that he rewards those who earnestly seek him.*" [14]

It is inherently irrational to believe that such a finely tuned,

---

[14] Hebrews 11:6 (NIV)

elaborate universe could appear on its own, regardless the length of time contemplated. How does "order" come from "disorder"? It doesn't, according to the second law of thermodynamics (or, *Entropy*), which Science firmly believes as an established *unchangeable* natural law. The law of *Entropy* states that things go from *Order* to *Disorder*, not from *Disorder* to *Order* such as the Big Bang theory attempts to suggest.

The Big Bang theory postulates a contradiction to science's own understanding of natural law. How long do you think you would stare at the desert sand before a computer would rise from it, even though all the elements that makes a computer exist there? How much more *irrational* is it to believe that something as amazing and exquisitely complex as our *universe* and the human form, ultimately came from nothing, much less exist in such a well-defined order, without a magnificent intelligent *Designer.*

Our universe is an intricately designed watch who had a watchmaker. The wisest man ever to live said this, *"wisdom laid out the foundations of the earth and heavens"* [15] If "wisdom" laid the foundation of our universe, then where did that "wisdom" come from? I once remarked to an agnostic friend who was mocking the idea of creation as coming from God. I said, "You and I both have great Faith; we both believe in an *"eternal something"*. I believe in an eternal God. You simply believe in *eternal matter.* You actually have more faith than I. You believe the universe just happened from nothing by some *unimaginable* cosmic event. It takes a lot of faith to believe matter has existed

---

[15] Proverbs 3: 19-20 (NIV)

here forever. You willingly accept the hypothesis that *"matter"* has always been, while rejecting, as feeble-minded, the idea that God has always existed. I believe in an original Source for my belief. As Atheists and Agnostics, you can point to no source for your belief.

I often ask an Atheist this question, "If a basic life form such as an amoeba was content to be an amoeba, what would cause it to want to be something else? It would have to have a source *"outside of itself"* to put pressure on it to become *something else*, would it not?" It would not inherently have such a drive to become anything else, even by chance without some kind of pressure, outside itself, pushing it toward something other than what it was originally. So I ask them, "What was that source? Water has always been water; it has never tried to be anything else but water. Since science states that water is the source of all life, why would that which science theorizes evolved out of, or from *water* seek to become something other than what water originally designed it to be? They have no answer.

Others argue that it took billions of years for our universe to form what it is now. They reject the idea that an Almighty God can create a "mature earth" with everything mankind would ever need to function in their environment. *Elohim* was not confined to simply creating a *baby earth* and wait billions of years for it to grow up. After all, *Elohim* created mature trees and vegetation with their seeds in them to continue reproducing. Why not a mature earth as well? For it is written: *"I will destroy the wisdom of the wise; the intelligence of the intelligent I will frustrate."* Where is the wise man? Where is *the scholar? Where is the philosopher of this age? Has not God made foolish the wisdom of the world?* [16] Why? Because human wisdom attempts to reach a conclusion outside the *divine,* to create what only a *divine* Creator could do.

Only God can create laws of the universe, scientists insist are *irrevocable* and fixed, and then create something else that defies scientifically based natural laws. Saturn has several moons; and all but one rotate the same way. One does not, but revolves around Saturn in the opposite direction. If gravity exists to compel a certain performance in a specific way universally, then such an event could never be explained by the universal laws of nature - apart from an omnipotent influencing source. God creates things that contradict these natural laws we know are fixed to show HE alone, is the Source of all things with unlimited power. God shows *His* awesome existence by setting specific laws in motion, and then defying them, so that mankind can clearly observe the existence of **Elohim** within the elegant majesty of His creation. It is written: *"He is before all things, and in him all things hold together."* [17]

The questions God asks of Job ultimately demand a conclusive answer of *divine* origin. God asks:

> *"Why do you confuse the issue?*
> *Why do you talk without knowing what you're*
> *talking about?*

---

[16] 1 Corinthians 1:19-20 (NIV)
[17] Colossians 1:17 (NIV)

I have some questions for you, and I want some
straight answers:

1. *Where were you when I created the earth?*
2. *Who decided on its size? Certainly you'll know that!*
3. *Who came up with the blueprints and measurements?*
4. *How was its foundation poured,*
5. *And who set the cornerstone?*
6. *And who took charge of the ocean*
   When it gushed forth like a baby from the womb?
   Then I made a playpen for it,
   A strong playpen so it couldn't run loose,
   And said, 'Stay here, this is your place.
   Your wild tantrums are confined to this place.'
7. *And have you ever ordered Morning, 'Get up!'*
   told Dawn, 'Get to work!'
   As the sun brings everything to light,
   brings out all the colors and shapes?
8. *Have you ever gotten to the true bottom of things,*
   explored the labyrinthine caves of deep ocean?
9. *Do you know where Light comes from*
   and where Darkness lives?
10. *Have you ever traveled to where snow is made,*
    seen the vault where hail is stockpiled?
    The arsenals of hail and snow that I keep in readiness?
11. *Can you find your way to where lightning is launched,*
    or to the place from which the wind blows?
12. *Who do you suppose carves canyons*

And who do you think is the father of rain and dew,
the mother of ice and frost?

13. *You don't for a minute imagine*
these marvels of weather just happen, do you?

14. *Can you catch the eye of the beautiful Pleiades sisters,*
or distract Orion from his hunt?

15. *Can you get Venus to look your way,*
or get the Great Bear and her cubs to come out and play?

16. *Do you know the first thing about the sky's constellations*
and how they affect things on Earth?

17. *Can you get the attention of the clouds,*
and commission a shower of rain?

18. *Can you take charge of the lightning bolts*
and have them report to you for orders?

19. *Who do you think gave weather-wisdom to the ibis,*
and storm-savvy to the rooster?

20. *Does anyone know enough to number all the clouds*
or tip over the rain barrels of heaven? [18]

With all the irrefutable evidence for a *divine* intelligent Creator, why do people go to such extreme efforts to "resist" the obvious evidence that there is an omnipotent Creator, a divine Source for everything that exists? It is written, *"But they deliberately forget that long ago by God's word the heavens existed and the earth was formed out of water and by water."* [19] It is also written, *"Instead of believing what they knew was the*

---

[18] Job 38: (The Message Bible)

[19] 2 Peter 3:5 (NIV)

truth about God, they deliberately chose to believe lies." [20] And again it is written, *"For although they knew God,*

> *they neither glorified him as God*
> *nor gave thanks to him,*
> *their thinking became futile,*
> *their foolish hearts were darkened."* [21]

J. B. Phillips translates it this way, *"since they considered themselves too high and mighty to acknowledge God, he allowed them to become (playthings) of their degenerate minds."* [22] And again, it is written, *"they show no regard for the works of the Lord and what His hands have done."*[23]

But there is much, much more to the Creation Story than simply having an omnipotent *divine* Creator expressing Himself and His unlimited power to create something from nothing. **Elohim** is a *Spirit* (invisible to the eye) who dwells in a Kingdom much more real than the physical world we occupy. Why? Because that Kingdom is eternal and not limited by time and space, or physical boundaries, or even the laws of nature and science. Mankind will always be left bewildered, scratching their heads to explain the contradictions of natural laws which exist in his universal world.

We've explored the incontrovertible fact that there has to be a Creator. Why? Because there is a "Creation" which

---

20 Romans 1:26 (Living Bible)

21 Romans 1:21 (NIV)

22 Romans 1:28 (J.B. Phillips Translation)

23 Psalms 28:5 (NIV)

exists well beyond mankind's imagination or comprehension. Our universe holds many secrets that modern science have only begun to scratch the surface on understanding. Only an intelligence well beyond the realm of *cosmic accident* is undeniably at work in our existence.

But what is all this vast creation for? And for whom? **Elohim** has something in mind. He calls them "humankind". This is where we pick up the story which ultimately brings us to the divine purpose of it all.

CHAPTER THREE

Why Create Humankind

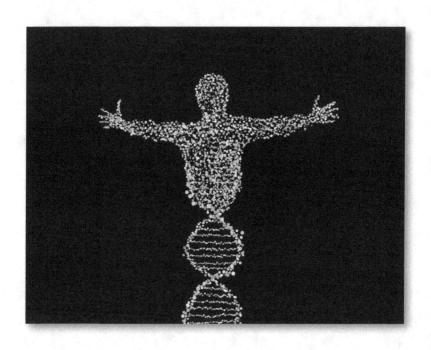

Why create mankind at all, if **Elohim** is all sufficient needing nothing? What was God thinking? And Why? Let's consider the possibility that God's initial creative act was to create the Heavens and the Earth followed by the creation of humankind to live on this elaborately appointed place called *Earth*. Is it not written? *"First this; God created the Heavens and Earth. All you see, all you don't see."* [24] Consider that humankind is at the "beginning" of God's creative story and not some distant after-thought; and therefore of utmost importance to God's divine intention. After all, is it not written that even angelic *beings*, although powerful, are created to serve at the Creator's pleasure for the benefit of humankind? Is it not written that, *"angels are spirit messengers sent out with the task to help and care for those who are to receive his salvation, ..."* [25]

Elohim is an eternal *"Spirit"* and after **Elohim** made Earth with all the trees, flowers, countless variety of insects and animals, He wanted to create a living "human-being" to lavish this vast goodness on. A kind of "God family", made in His own likeness and image to enjoy what He had made and to have fellowship with. **Elohim**, in fact, made "humankind" in His own image. For it is written: ." *God created human beings; he created them godlike, Reflecting God's nature. He created them male and female."* [26] And what was that image and "likeness"? It was a created "spirit" (or, *spirit being*) which HE called humankind, *male* and *female*. It is written, *"He has made everything beautiful*

---

[24] Genesis 1:1 (The Message Bible)

[25] Hebrews 1: 14 (Living Bible)

[26] Genesis 1:27 (The Message Bible)

in its time. He has also set eternity in the human heart; yet no one can fathom what God has done from beginning to end". [27] And again *"there is a spirit in man, and the breath of the Almighty gives him understanding."* [28]

First God created a *"spirit human being"* made in His own image and in His likeness. Then in Genesis 2, God "forms" the first man a body from the "dust of the ground" and placed the *spirit-man* into that body. Mankind was a created *"spirit being"* before he became housed as a *"physical-body living-soul being".* The *spirit-man* now had a body fully expressive, fully spirit and fully human with a voice and a way of expressing himself, his emotions, thoughts, imaginations dreams; and even the ability to turn his imaginations into tangible reality.

The Psalmist so eloquently and poetically describes these events when he writes:

"Oh yes, you shaped me first inside, then out;
you formed me in my mother's womb.
I thank you, High God—you're breathtaking!
Body and soul, I am marvelously made!
I worship in adoration—what a creation!
You know me inside and out,
you know every bone in my body;
You know exactly how I was made, bit by bit,
how I was sculpted from nothing into something.

---

[27] Ecclesiastes 3:11 (NIV)
[28] Job 32:8 (NKIV)

Like an open book, you watched me grow from conception to birth;

all the stages of my life were spread out before you." [29]

And what a creation humankind is! It would take volumes of libraries to describe all the intricacies of the human form of *male* and *female*, and their corresponding "spiritual" characteristics and how these "intertwine" to make a "living soul". Science suggests that the human brain is capable of making 20 million-billion actions per second. Evolutionists argue that humans *evolved* from monkeys, or even lower life forms. I reject the absurdity of that idea. You can teach a monkey to use a hammer, but you can't teach a monkey to "make a modern one".

Only "humankind", made in the image of God, possesses the ability to imagine things not yet reality and create intricate machines from his own imagination, from the substances his environment provides. Have you ever seen a monkey mine coal, make steel, create an automobile or airplane, or make a rocket go to the moon and back? How about performing open heart surgery or make a microchip, computer or telephone? God made humankind to think, speak, imagine, and then achieve their greatest imagination by being "creative" just like **Elohim** who gave them those attributes.

God had to create. It is His nature and that nature to create was also placed in the *"spirit-being"* called humankind. It is our nature to create as well, because the essence of mankind's nature began from God's own essence.

---

[29] Psalm 139:13-16 (The Message Bible)

CHAPTER FOUR

Why Create a Physical Body

I f the "invisible spiritual" world is more "real" than the physical one: Why then, did God create a physical world at all? And why take humankind from a *spirit* being to embody that of a physical being?

Let's look at the physical body: What an amazing ingenious work of art; a miraculous creative phenomena that baffles modern science to this very day. The human being embraces both "physical and spiritual" components neatly intertwined, so delicate and yet so resilient. One part cannot function without the other. Our spiritual part needs a way to express itself; our physical form needs a life giving force to make it work. Such is the creative union of humankind. The "spirit" must have "expression", the words spoken, the gestures of the hands, a laugh or smile, the multifaceted facial expression, the tender caress, all give our *spirit* meaningful expression and consciousness.

In original intent, each cell of our body was designed to live forever. The body was never designed to decay or die. Even in our fallen state, the body will go to great lengths to survive, endure inextricable circumstances and pull itself back from the brink of death. Why? It must survive! Our *spirit* "demands" it. Why? Because something inside humankind seeks the eternal, to survive in a body fully functional and fully "expressive" in every way.

Humankind, in a physical world needs to see, hear, speak, touch, taste, feel and experience - to fully "express itself". The *spirit*, although the core of one's being, cannot show what is there without some way to "express" it. So, God gave humans the ability to express themselves by giving them a body and do it with. Humans have a mind to think, a voice to speak, hands to hold things and feet to freely move about. All this gives humans full expression to all that their *spirit* gives birth to. We know that one of the frustrations endured by the deaf, is the inability to give full "voice" and expression of their feelings. Even when no one is around, we humans find ourselves "speaking or laughing to ourselves", giving full expression to the *spirit* within us that prompts those utterances.

Our "spirit" can't speak, or express its feelings, make its thoughts known or emotions felt. No, it needs a "body" to do all that. The ability to express feelings in a physical way, speak, etc., is the consciousness from which we live and thrive. Sometimes, God has even granted angelic beings, who are normally *"ministering spirits,"* [30] the ability to take on physical forms. Why? Just so they could connect with mankind in his physical world with the message they carried. We know that angels, taking on a physical form forcibly removed Lot and his family out of Sodom. Angels grabbed the hand of Abraham just before he thrust the knife into his son Isaac and an angel in a physical form, wrestled all night with Jacob. Our "spirit" needs to be able to express what it feels, so God made a body so that when united with our *spirit*, we become *"human/spirit beings"* and fully expressive.

---

[30] Hebrews 1:14 (NIV)

CHAPTER FIVE

Why God Created Laws and Boundaries

Although mankind at its core is a "spiritual-being", an act of disobedience changed everything in mankind's physical world. Have you ever asked yourself: Why did God put a tree in the Garden of Eden and then tell the man and woman NOT to eat of it? Why put the temptation there at all? We should then reason! If there were no "boundaries", we would not know there is a God. After all, God created the world with boundaries and set laws to govern everything. The tides can only go so far and then must retreat again. The Earth is not some nomad wandering aimless across the heavens. No, it has a specific circuit, to which the Earth takes a constant course, to govern seasons and times. Science refers to these governing principles as "universal laws". Things like gravity, although we can't fully explain it, we know it exists as a constant in our physical world. God set these boundaries so that when HE acts outside of them, we know beyond any doubt there is a higher divine "presence" at work that transcends explanation of the world we know. By these unexplainable events, we know there is God and there is no denying His existence.

Adam and Eve were given "boundaries" and instructions to insure their happiness. Mankind without set boundaries to govern their behavior can do no wrong, regardless the result or consequences of that behavior. God is Good. Why? Because He can be nothing else. Mankind was given boundaries and the ability to choose. With boundaries, you can choose either to do the right thing or the wrong thing; to do "good" or to do "evil". You can either choose to be the person God created you to be or you can choose to be something else outside of His divine purpose and design.

Another thing boundaries tell us is, whether or not we will honor the One who established those boundaries as having our best interests at heart or, will we view them, as Adam and Eve ultimately did, that *"God is holding out on us"* and *"we deserve to have that."* Adam and Eve thought, *"We deserve it and God's not giving it to us"*. Of course, we all know how that decision turned out. Mankind wanted to have the *"knowledge"* of both *"good* and *evil"* and so disobeyed **Elohim**'s boundary. Humankind now has that "knowledge".

Humanity now lives in a world filled with both "good and evil". Look at what the world has become with that knowledge of good and evil. Many argue, if **Elohim** is so Good, then why does He "allow" such evil to occur in the earth? Mankind must take responsibility for the evil that plagues their earthly existence. Evil consequence was not God's design, it was mankind's doing. God only wanted humankind to know "good" and *never* "evil". It was *we humans* who wanted the "knowledge" of evil as well as the knowledge of good. And since earth is mankind's domain to decide: WE GOT OUR WISH!

When **Elohim** made humans, He placed them in a perfect environment that was "ALL GOOD". In fact, the human body is not designed to handle stress and negative events or feelings. The body has no mechanism to handle negative emotions or negative stress. When stressed or negatively impacted, the body actually produces an overabundance of good hormones that then have a negative impact on the body and psyche.

Carolyn Leaf, a highly respected neuro-scientist has done major neurological studies on this phenomenon showing that humans were never wired for the negative or stress environment.

Elohim's original design of the human form did not include mechanisms for evil in their world; and so He gave mankind a "boundary" to protect the "Good" He had created. If humans kept the terms of the *boundary*, nothing *evil* would befall them. If mankind crossed that boundary, *irreversible* consequences lay within that disobedience. *Elohim* was to be mankind's source for everything good. However, with the violation of *Elohim*'s protective boundary, evil now entered the picture separating mankind from all things good given him by His Creator. Mankind no longer has "all things good". Mankind now lives in the world of both "good and evil".

Humankind had been created for meaningful relationship with *Elohim*. With the introduction of "disobedience", that connection with *Elohim* was broken. However, the insatiable need of humankind to connect still remained. How would humanity deal with this "disconnect" with their Creator. Humans must cling to something, but what?

CHAPTER SIX

Why Humans Need to Connect

So great is humankind's need to connect that even when we speak to someone on the phone for the first time, we tend to take his or her voice and put a mental picture of what we imagine that person looks like. Why? Just so we can connect with the voice in a meaningful way. We need a body in order to connect. Is it any wonder why technologies like, Facebook, Skype, YouTube, and others are universally used in social media. We humans must connect, we have too. It is inextricably hard-wired in our psyche and physiological makeup. Our "being" demands connection.

An experiment was reportedly conducted in 1944 in the United States on 40 newborn infants to determine whether individuals could thrive alone on basic physiological needs without affection. The newborn infants had caregivers who would feed them, bathe them and change their diapers. Caregivers had been instructed not to interact with the babies more than was necessary. All their physical needs were attended to. However, the study was quickly halted after four months. Half of the babies had died. There was no physiological cause for the deaths; for they were all physically very healthy. Before each baby died, there was a period where they would stop verbalizing and trying to engage their caregivers, and just stop moving, never cry or change expression. Death followed shortly. The Study concluded that the need for nurturing touch is vital to our survival and well-being.

Aloneness and perpetual solitude is not an environment in which humans can survive or thrive in. This is why isolation is considered one of the worst forms of torture - mentally, emotionally and physically. Studies also show that married couple's life spans are statistically longer than singles because of that constant connection of touch and interaction with another human that is so vital to the human experience.

Humans go to great lengths to make connection. Although humorous, the movie "Castaway" with Tom Hanks depicts just how far humans will go to have connection. Tom Hanks, marooned from a crash-landing, imagined the personage of a volleyball he endearingly referred to as "WILSON" as his companion. It clearly demonstrates humans will talk to just about anything in order to make a connection; even if it is volleyball. We are created for connection and we will find it one way or another, even if it is only imaginary.

CHAPTER SEVEN

Why Adam Left God for Eve

Genesis tells the story of how **Elohim** made Adam the first man. After this, God asked Adam to name all the animals He had created before He created Adam. Ever wondered why God gave Adam the responsibility to name everything in his earthly physical world? God made Adam to be Ruler of Earth. Earth was made for man, and his unique "domain" of authority. It is written: (God spoke): *"Let us make human beings in our image, make them reflecting our nature So they can be responsible for the fish in the sea, the birds in the air, the cattle, And, yes, Earth itself, and every animal that moves on the face of Earth." God created human beings; he created them godlike, Reflecting God's nature. He created them male and female."* [31]

After naming all the animals, Adam was the only one without a corresponding mate. Out of everything God made, the only time God said something wasn't good, was when He said, *"it was not good for man to be alone."* [32] So **Elohim** put Adam to sleep and took a rib from his side and formed a woman as an equal companion. They would populate and rule the world together. That was God's original intent and mankind's original position.

Satan, who once helped rule God's vast expanse of the universe was thrown out of his high position because of the sin of wicked "pride". The scripture tells us Satan was thrown down to earth where another of God's creation was in charge and, to which Satan would now be "subservient". This was Mankind's domain and humans were King of the Earth and

---

[31] Genesis 1:26-27 (The Message Bible)

[32] Genesis 2:18 (NIV)

Satan was homeless, a mere "vagabond", wandering trespasser, without anything or any authority there. So Satan set out to steal the kingdom humans ruled for themselves and used the one *boundary* God gave mankind to take the dominion called Earth from them as told in Genesis chapter 3.

Have you ever wondered why Adam "deliberately" ate the fruit with Eve in "knowing" disobedience? For it is written, *"Adam was not deceived."* [33] He knew exactly what he was doing when he ate the forbidden fruit, and Adam knew it was wrong, even if Eve did not.

We must examine how God set things up in order to discover Why Adam chose Eve over staying in the Garden with Spirit-**Elohim**. When God brought Eve to Adam, Adam exclaimed; *"bone of my bone, flesh of my flesh."* [34] Then God finished Adam's sentence by saying, *"for this reason a man shall leave his father and mother and be united to his wife."* [35] When presented with the woman, it was love at first sight. Adam immediately gravitated to Eve. Why? Because now he could be fully expressive with her through sight, sound, voice, touch and communication of his body, soul and spirit with her's, in every way. He could not do that with *Spirit-***Elohim**.

So why would Adam choose to leave God and the perfect Garden for Eve knowing that death would be the consequences of his disobedience? Why? Because Eve was someone he could see, touch, embrace and fully express himself with, while

---

[33] 1 Timothy 2:14 (NIV)
[34] Genesis 2:23 (NIV)
[35] Genesis 2:24 (NIV)

Elohim was a "voice" a *Spirit* walking with him in the Garden. God was not someone Adam could touch, embrace, and fully connect with, nor receive the same kind of full expression in return.

Adam never said of God, *"bone of my bone, flesh of my flesh"* even though God had breathed into Adam His own essence. Adam clung to Eve over God, because love needs a way of expressing itself. LOVE NEEDS A BODY to communicate a complete connection. Without a body, the expression of love is just an intangible abstract concept. And when the time came to decide whether to stay with Spirit-*Elohim,* or leave with Eve, Adam did exactly what God said Adam would do, Adam left his Father and Mother (Spirit-*Elohim*) and united himself to his wife.

When the choice to stay with an "invisible" God which Adam couldn't see or touch, verses sharing whatever existence lie ahead with someone he could fully express himself with, Adam "willingly and knowingly" shared in Eve's disobedience with "full knowledge" of its consequences. To Adam, the need to be fully expressive with another was infinitely more powerful than the lure of the Garden with a God he couldn't see or fully know. Do you think Adam loved God? Of course he did. But the ability to fully express himself and communicate love in the spiritual/physical sense with Eve outweighed the drive for eternal life without the ability to fully express himself to his *Spirit* Creator.

The idea of being able to "fully express" one's self to another has been the source of mythological love stories for centuries.

These stories compel the tale of gods who leave their place of deity to become a man or woman and the ability to touch, speak and love. Why? Because LOVE NEEDS A BODY to show what the *spirit* wants to express. I am reminded of King-Emperor Edward VIII who gave up the thrown of the British Empire in 1936, including his position as Emperor of India to marry a woman, Wallis Simpson, whom he loved more than the seat of power. Power has its exhilaration and privilege, but it cannot take the place of true connection of the heart and soul with another human.

Even the murdering Cain, after killing his brother Abel, was so afraid of total isolation and abandonment from all other human contact that he pleaded with **Elohim** that this burden was too heavy to bare. God agreed and put a mark on him so others would not kill him or shun him in total abandonment. Cain was also provided a wife he could hold on to and learn something of what love was about.

We can see humanity's insatiable longing for connection through the myriad of love songs over the centuries. They convey such a longing and deep seeded need to connect, that many of these songs attribute "divine qualities" to another human as an expression of just how strong this desire for connection and companionship is. But nowhere is it more eloquently portrayed than in the Songs of Solomon. These songs portray a graphic illustration of love and the need for connection of body, soul and spirit; and depict humankind's deepest longings for companionship. Solomon concludes his elaborately detailed songs between his lover and he with these words.

I am my lover's.
I'm all he wants. I'm all the world to him!
Come, dear lover—
Hang my locket around your neck,
wear my ring on your finger.
Love is invincible facing danger and death.
Passion laughs at the terrors of hell.
The fire of love stops at nothing—
it sweeps everything before it.
Flood waters can't drown love,
torrents of rain can't put it out.
Love can't be bought, love can't be sold—
it's not to be found in the marketplace.[36]

As so eloquently expressed by Solomon, it is our deepest need to connect with another human being. When Adam left the Garden with Eve, it was because of this deep and insatiable need to connect. God being a "Spirit-being", a connection on all three levels of body, soul and spirit was impossible. In this physical world of mankind, there has to be a body to satisfy this "tri-unity" of mankind's existence. And so the story continues to unfold, as Spirit-**Elohim** would bridge the gap between the "spiritual world" and the "natural physical world", in order to connect with humankind on their most deepest need levels. Spirit-**Elohim**'s desire and mankind's deepest need gave birth to what has become known as the Greatest Love Story Ever Told.

---

[36] Song of Solomon 8:6-8 (The Message Bible)

CHAPTER EIGHT

Why Love From a Distance Didn't Work

Bette Midler sings a Song; *"God is watching you from a distance."* We are familiar with what *"love from a distance"* looks like. A disaster happens some place and we as concerning people give money to buy things to help from a sense of care and compassion. The disaster doesn't really affect our lives directly or cause us personal pain. Why? "Compassion from a distance" isn't really what you could call love in its purest form. We aren't in the trenches where the pain is. We aren't acquainted with the human trauma and misery *"up close and personal"*. Only those who are on the front line actually feel the "pain" of others, the suffering, the agony, the bewilderment, the confusion, the struggle to survive. In the trenches is where it becomes personal, a part of you; where your soul is joined to it and your heart aches right alongside with others.

In the Old Testament, Spirit-**Elohim** looks down on man "from a distance." He sees their struggles and pain and sends "aid" time and again. Manna from heaven when they were hungry, water from a rock when they were thirsty. But their struggles did not affect HIM directly. God did not share in their human weaknesses, tragedy, or their painful struggles. In fact, we find **Elohim** saying, *"If I were hungry, I would not tell you."* [37] Why? All creation, and more, was readily at His disposal. And if it wasn't there; voila! He spoke it into existence. Spirit-**Elohim** lacked nothing and needed nothing. Oh yes, God recognized that man was dust, but He still didn't share their pain, struggles or their fear of death. The fear of death was that dark abyss that

---

[37] Psalms 50:12 (NIV)

lie just beyond mankind's fleeting life-span; that nothingness of "non-existence" that lay just ahead of his last breathe.

When Satan approached God about Job, God was not hesitant to permit Satan to inflict varying degrees of pain and suffering on Job. Sure, God was confident that Job would not deny Him to the point of no redemption. But God was not a "party to the pain and suffering" Job was going through. We find Job faltering under the confusion of where God was in all his suffering. Job was not perfect in his responses either. We find Job complains that God does not understand and there was no justice in all he was enduring. Although the story ends well with God restoring Job to greater wealth and position than before his ordeal with Satan, Spirit-*Elohim* was still "watching from a distance" and wasn't really in the trenches with Job sharing the experience with him. He is the One and only God, a *Spirit*, having need of nothing. *Elohim* was God and that was that. He could be nothing else.

Moses was called *"a Friend of God,"* but God, although angered and disappointed with Israel, was not a direct party to the enormous daily task Moses had and the overwhelming frustration that caused Moses to lose patience and strike the rock when he should have just spoken to it. Can you imagine how Moses felt in all this? He was given a law he knew the children of Israel would not follow. Imagine yourself being saddled with a task you knew you couldn't complete, but if you didn't complete it, the punishment is pain, suffering and ultimately death lie just ahead of you. This is why it was written of mankind, *"who all their lives were held in slavery by their fear of death."* [38]

Ancient history is filled with divine exploits of an Almighty God. Spirit-***Elohim*** could thunder from heaven, He could push back the Red Sea with His breathe so that His people could walk on dry ground, He could rain down the most tasty food, He could stop the sun in its tracks, He could even show loving kindness, mercy, faithfulness, patience and longsuffering and compassion toward humankind, but Spirit-***Elohim*** could not directly express Love up close and personal in a sense humans could relate to or understand in their physical world. Even with Moses, God's chosen messenger, Spirit-***Elohim*** had to shield himself so that Moses could at least get a peek at God's majestic essence without being destroyed in the process.

In ancient times, when ***Elohim*** attempted to speak to humans, it terrified them. Mankind ran from the *Voice* of God, rather than were drawn to it. When Spirit-***Elohim*** manifested Himself it appeared as a pillar of *consuming* fire or an ominous billowing cloud of dark smoke. Ezekiel said he fell down like a dead man just simply gazing on God's glory in the form of a cloud. ***Elohim*** had to write the Ten Commandments with His own finger on physical stone tablets just so mankind could understand what He wanted from them. In ancient times, we see time and time again that Spirit-***Elohim*** used His creation to reveal Himself because He *"had no body."* Mankind could *"not*

---

look upon God and live." [39] So Spirit-*Elohim* shielded Himself by using prophets, Kings and Priests to do His bidding for Him. Even at their best, an imperfect man could not effectively communicate what God wanted humanity to know about Himself, or the Love *Elohim* really wanted to show to His human family.

Neither prophets, Priests or Seers had the ability to show how much God loved His human creation. Why? Because it wasn't perfect Love and perfect Love needs a perfect body to reveal it. None was available, no not even one. *Elohim* could wipe away huge armies in one wave of His little finger, He could give visions of the future, stop the sun in its tracks, turn the universe upside down, but He could not, as a Spirit, express love in its deepest, purest and most perfect form in a way humankind could understand or respond to, from the distance of His majesty and awesomeness of His Throne.

Imagine yourself only a *spirit*. What would you do? How would you do it? You might move objects, move through walls, ride on the wind, smile at the bitter cold, but you could never feel the warmth of a fire, the companionship of another, laugh out loud, take the hand of a friend, hold a newborn baby or weep with joy at the beauty all around you. Why? Because you need a body to do all that.

You might say: doesn't the scriptures tell us that, "they that worship *Elohim* must worship Him in "spirit and truth."? This is true with worship. But you cannot love merely in "spirit" alone. Love must be tangibly expressed for another to know

---

[39] Exodus 33:20 (NIV)

it's true value. It cannot merely be felt, it must be "expressed". Otherwise, it is incomplete, and therefore, just a feeling; an abstract emotion and not real enough to be complete in its intention. Without a body, the perfect expression of love is not possible.

CHAPTER NINE

Why a Messiah

D o you think Spirit-*Elohim*, who fills the universe and beyond, would leave Himself without means of expression beyond the trappings of creation? *Elohim's* love for His human family was so infinite that HE must show his human family just how much HE really, really loved them. Sure, the ancient scrolls reveal again and again that God's love is from everlasting to everlasting, but who could know it? And how could it be shown in a way humans could understand and connect with? God "telling" us He loved us was an abstract concept without the one necessary ingredient of meaningful connection; that of "touch".

Spirit-*Elohim* did not intend to just show mercy, kindness, compassion, caring, and healing from a distance. His intention was to connect with mankind on his deepest need level, in a way that humanity could truly know how much *Elohim* loves His human family. He was not content to simply tell us He loves us; God wanted to show love completely by getting down into the trenches of life with us and alongside us. Why? Because LOVE MUST HAVE A BODY.

This is why it is written that Jesus (Yeshua) the Christ, was in the mind of God from the beginning foundation of the world, long before Spirit-*Elohim* made the first human. It is written: *"Long before he laid down earth's foundations, he had us in mind, had settled on us as the focus of his love, to be made whole and holy by his love. Long, long ago he decided to adopt us into his family through Jesus Christ. (What pleasure he took in planning this!) He wanted us to enter into the celebration of his lavish gift-giving by the hand of his beloved Son."* [40] God

---

[40] Ephesians 1:2-5 (The Message Bible)

purposed to make Himself known; to take on a form *{from a pure manifested human seed reflecting His complete divine character}* which could express incomprehensible Love. God is Love, but Love must be "expressed" in a physical tangible way to be complete for humans to truly know it.

God taking on the human expression was more than simply the means to the end. Spirit-*Elohim* wanted to fully express Himself to all humanity He had given life to; to share every experience of humans, to hear Himself laugh with them, cry with them, share feelings of companionship with them, have friendship with them, touching them, holding and healing them and finally, "loving them up close and personal" in a way that there would never be any question or doubt that *Elohim*'s love was visible. God couldn't do all that with mankind fully, simply as an eternal unapproachable *Spirit*, but He could if He made a Body for Himself to dwell in. The invisible Spirit-*Elohim*, by making Himself visible through a Body, could get right down with us in the trenches of life and communicate completely in ways we humans could understand and connect with.

An eye-witness to the Messiah reveals just how the eternal Spirit *Elohim* would make Himself known. *"No one has ever seen God, but the one and only Son, who is Himself God and is in closest relationship with the Father, has made Him known."* [41] The way Spirit-*Elohim* would embody a human form would be a masterful miracle as spectacular as mankind could ever imagine. It would have to be as divine as His essence, yet the end result would have to be, that His presence here would be

[41] John 1:18 (NIV Readers Edition)

both fully human and yet fully God. HE would be human in that He would taste completely and fully the human experience while at the same time, expressing the complete essence of His divine identity. How would this be accomplished you ask?

CHAPTER TEN

Why a Miraculous Birth

There was only one way Spirit-*Elohim* could make His human creation understand the breadth, length, depth and height of His infinite Love for them. He would have to make Himself a "Body". Why? Because LOVE MUST HAVE A BODY to fully express the essence of Love. Spirit-*Elohim* would have to come to the world as ONE OF US, but HE would have to have a "sinless body" because a pure and Holy *Elohim* could not embody Himself in sinful flesh. So God designed His entrance by the most elaborate display of creativity imaginable. *Elohim* is a Spirit, so the Body He would take could not come in the usual way of human procreation. It would have to be a *divine* entrance and this body would be known as the *Son of God*. Why? Because His Body would be both completely human and completely Spirit *Elohim*.

Elohim foretold of this miraculous entrance in Genesis when He said, *"the seed of the woman,"* [42] not the seed of the man, would be the His divine entrance. This would be how *Elohim* would crush Satan's hold over humanity's earthly domain. The *"sins of the fathers"* [43] are always passed down to the children. Therefore, the prophet uttered the words on how *Elohim* would accomplish a sinless body for Himself: *"The virgin is going to have a baby. She will give birth to a son. And he will be called Immanuel." The name Immanuel means "God with us."* [44]

When God decided to come in person to make Himself and His love fully known to His human family, what did God do?

---

[42] Genesis 3:15 (New King James)

[43] Numbers 14:18 (NKJV)

[44] Isaiah 7:14 (NIV)

He said. *"Sacrifice and offering you did not desire, but a body you prepared for me."* [45] Then (**Elohim**) said, *"Here I am, it is written about me in the scroll, I have come to do your will, O God."* [46] And again, *"Beyond all question, the mystery of godliness (godhead) is great. He [spirit-**Elohim**-God] appeared in a body."* [47]

Elohim longed to show His love to His children up close and personal. So the prophet Isaiah reveals **Elohim**'s divine entrance in this way:

"For to us a child is born,
    to us a son is given,
and the government will be on his shoulders.
    And he will be called
Wonderful Counselor, Mighty God,
    Everlasting Father, Prince of Peace.
Of the greatness of his government and peace
    there will be no end.
He will reign on David's throne
    and over his kingdom,
establishing and upholding it
    with justice and righteousness
from that time on and forever.
    The zeal of the Lord Almighty
will accomplish this." [48]

---

[45] Hebrews 10:4 (NIV)

[46] Psalm 40:6-8 / Hebrews 10:5] (NIV)

[47] 1 Timothy 3:16 (NIV)

[48] Isaiah 9:6-8 (NIV)

Is it any wonder that Paul writes of the *Tri-unity* of God to the Colossians in this manner; "He (Christ), *"appeared in a body …. is the image of the invisible God, the firstborn over all creation. For by Him all things were created, things in heaven and on earth, visible and invisible, whether thrones or powers or rulers or authorities; all things were created by Him and for Him. He is before all things, and in Him all things hold together."* [49] To the Church at Rome it is written: *"from them* (the Jews) *is traced the <u>human</u> ancestry of Christ, who is God over all"*[50] And finally Paul writes: *"For in Christ there is all of God in a human body."* [51]

This is why Messiah (Yeshua the Christ) repeatedly makes the discourse of who He really was to His disciples as well as to us, *"I and the Father are one"* (or, one and the same). Jesus said, *"believe the miracles, that you may know and understand that the Father is in me, and I in the Father."* [52] Jesus goes on to say, *"If you really know me, you would know my Father as well. From now on, you do know Him and have seen Him."* Philip asks, "Lord, show us the Father and that will be enough for us." Jesus answered: *"Don't you know me, Philip, even after I have been among you such a long time? Anyone who has seen me has seen the Father. How can you say, 'Show us the Father'? Don't you believe that I am in the Father, and that the Father is in me? The words I say to you I do not speak on my own authority. Rather, it is the Father, living in me, who is doing His work. Believe me*

---

[49] Colossians 1:15-17, 19) (NIV)
[50] Romans 9:5 (NIV)
[51] Colossians 2:9 (Living Bible)
[52] John 10:38,40 (NIV)

when I say that I am in the Father and the Father is in me." [53]
Messiah the Christ, goes on to say, *"the Son* (human) *can do nothing by Himself; He can do only what He sees His Father doing, because whatever the Father does the Son also does."* [54]

Paul shows us so clearly, the "Tri-unity" of **Elohim**'s manifestations when he writes, *"For God was pleased to have all his fullness dwell in him,* (in the body-Christ) *and through him (the body-Christ) to reconcile to himself all things, whether things on earth or things in heaven, by making peace through his blood, shed on the cross."* [55]

---

[53] John 14:7-11 (NIV)
[54] John 5:19 (NIV)
[55] Colossians 1:19-20 (NIV)

CHAPTER ELEVEN

Why *Elohim* Took on the Form of a Man

*E**lohim*** had originally placed Adam, as King, in charge of the Earth to subdue it and rule over it as the supreme authority of his environment. But when Adam and Eve sinned in disobedience, mankind lost "ownership" of the Earth they once ruled. Satan became the ruler of Earth's' principalities in mankind's place. Satan had been cast out of his position of authority with no place to go, and no kingdom of his own to rule. Satan thought if he could steal mankind's kingdom and position of authority, he would be taking something that ultimately belonged to God for himself.

And so, since a "man" (Adam) lost the Earthly kingdom he once dominated, a "man" (Jesus the human Christ- Son of God) as a man, would have to take it back from Satan. But not just any man, but a "sinless one". And since there is no one sinless but Spirit-*Elohim*, God would have to "do the job" Himself. The scriptures describe it this way, *"Since the children have flesh and blood, He too shared in their humanity."* [56]

You see: in ancient times, Spirit-*Elohim* could see man's pain and suffering, but He couldn't feel it. So Spirit-*Elohim* made Himself a body, put His Fullness in that body, *"For God was pleased to have all His fullness dwell in Him."* [57] And again, *"For in Christ all the fullness of the Deity lives in bodily form."* [58] *Elohim* then introduced himself to the world, in the likeness of a man as the *Son of God* to connect with humanity within his earthly understanding. For it is written, *"The Word became*

---

[56] Hebrews 2:14,15 (NIV)

[57] Colossians 1:19 (NIV)

[58] Colossians 2: 9 (NIV)

flesh and made his dwelling among us."[59] A "man" being, fully God and fully human, would take back dominion of the Earth and dislodge Satan once and for all as the ruling lord of the Earth. Mankind's world was lost by one man's sin {Adam}, and by one man's, sinless life, {Messiah Christ] snatched it back for those to whom it rightfully belonged. For it is written: *"just as sin entered the world through one man, and death through sin, and in this way death came to all men, because all sinned ... how much more did God's grace and the gift that came by the grace of the one man, Jesus Christ, overflow to the many!"* [60]

Once Messiah Christ had accomplished the full redemption of mankind's domain, taking back ALL that had been lost, (Yeshua the Christ) then declared to His believing family in a metaphoric decree, *"I have given you authority to trample on snakes and scorpions and to overcome all the power of the enemy; nothing will harm you."* [61]

But this was not **Elohim's** only redemptive act as Messiah Christ. **Elohim** had one other order of business to take care of. He wanted to show humankind the sacrifice He was willing to make, to show them just how much He loved His human creation. With a body, Spirit-**Elohim** could now express the "full measure" of His love and devotion to His human family up close and personal.

It is written how **Elohim**'s Love expressed itself in this Body called Messiah -Christ (Son of God). **Elohim**, in a body,

---

[59] John 1:14 (NIV)

[60] I Corinthians 5:12,15 (NIV)

[61] Luke 10:19 (NIV)

hugged us, laughed with us, cried with us, ate with us, endured hardship, was ridiculed, humiliated, falsely accused, mistreated, and utterly betrayed. Why? He became like one of us in every way so He could demonstrate up close and personal, one to one, LOVE in its purest form. No longer was Spirit-*Elohim* some abstract invisible concept, moving creation at will, showing his ominous power, but still unapproachable, "untouchable". Now we could see Him, touch Him, walk and talk with Him, actually be with Him.

Imagine, the God of the universe taking on the form of a human, and as the scriptures reflect, *"That which was from the beginning, which we have heard, which we have seen with our eyes, which we have looked at and our hands have touched, this we proclaim concerning the Word of life. The life appeared; we have seen it and testify to it, and we proclaim to you the eternal life, which was with the Father and has appeared to us."* [62]

When the (God-man Jesus Christ) appeared in a body, He began to demonstrate His boundless Love to humanity. It is written, *"God anointed Jesus of Nazareth with the Holy Spirit and power, and how He went around doing good and healing all who were under the power of the devil."* [63] Then the God-man did one more thing to let everyone know, beyond any question the full extent of His Love. God used the body He prepared for Himself to absorb all the sins, sickness, disease, mental illness, sorrow, pain and hopelessness into His prepared sinless body. He shed His sinless blood on the cross to take away all

[62] I John 1:1,2 (NIV)
[63] Act 10:38 (NIV)

those sins, and to make sure that Satan could never again steal the humans **Elohim** loves. This is why it is written, *"God so LOVED the world that He gave his one and only Son {the physical representation of Elohim} so that we would not perish, but have eternal life."* [64] **Elohim** is a *Spirit* and used a human body to reveal His boundless love to connect with humanity in a way humans could relate to and understand.

Jesus Christ the Messiah came, *"in the likeness of man to be a sin offering."* But why? In order to *"condemn sin"* and *"to destroy sin's control over us."* [65] And to seek and save all that was lost destroying all the works of darkness created by the fall of mankind in the Garden. Why? Because LOVE needed to be expressed in every way, to the fullest extent of suffering so that there would never be any question just how great **Elohim's** Love was for humanity, and how far God would go to show this infinite Love to His most valuable creation.

Nowhere in the scriptures is there any indication that Spirit-**Elohim** ever lowered Himself to serve angels. But **Elohim**, in the form of a man (Christ Jesus) humbled Himself to the lowest place possible to serve humanity's innermost deepest needs. He said, *"the Son of Man did not come to be served, but to serve, and to give his life as a ransom for many."* [66] Though **Elohim's** majesty is beyond description, His authority unequaled, ruling the heavens with a mighty display of power, **Elohim** demonstrated His indescribable LOVE by kneeling down in

---

[64] John 3:16 (NIV)

[65] Romans 8:3 (NIV)

[66] Matthew 20:28 (NIV)

front of humans to wash their feet and to call them His friends. *Elohim*, the God-man (Jesus Christ), who bows to serve no angelic being, and to which *"every knee in heaven and earth will bow to confess that He is supreme Lord,"* [67] set His outer garments aside, picked up a towel and basin of water, bowed Himself to the lowest position possible to serve the humans He loved so much, and to wash men's feet. Why? Because, LOVE MUST HAVE A BODY and, so LOVE, so indescribably, that it is beyond human words, knelt before his human creation to serve them. And as He did, Yeshua-Jesus the Christ spoke these enduring and eternal words, *"Greater love has no one than this; that he lay down his life for his friends."* [68]

When Jesus saw the multitude and knew they were hungry, He had "compassion" on them. Not simply compassion as one who would feel sorry for someone else's circumstances or condition from a distance, but one who knew hunger up close and personal. In a body, *Elohim* was one of "us" and truly knew the plight of need, and wrenched in His "gut" which means His emotions were tied to His physical body with an ability of full human expression. Jesus knew very well what hunger and deprivation was like. He had spent forty days and nights without food, while being tempted by Satan all along the way. The book of Hebrews describes it in this fashion, *"For this reason He had to be made like His brothers in every way, in order that He might become a merciful and faithful high priest,"* and *"Because He Himself suffered when He was tempted, He is*

---

[67] Romans 14:11 (NIV)
[68] John 15:13 (NIV)

able to help those who are being tempted." [69] And again, *"For we do not have a high priest who is unable to sympathize with our weaknesses, but we have one who has been tempted in every way, (shared fully in all our experiences) just as we are yet was without sin."* [70]

In this way **Elohim**, as Messiah Son of God, *"the radiance of God's glory and the exact representation of his being"* [71] and *"the image of the invisible God"* [72] felt as we feel, knew what we as humans experience and thereby, demonstrated His mercy and compassion to the fullest expression of Love this world has ever seen. LOVE had to have a "Body" to experience all that is human; to know the joy of victory and the agony of suffering. John writes, *"Having loved His own who were in the world, He now showed them the full extent of His love."* [73] How? By indescribable pain and suffering, by shedding His sinless blood to save ours.

Elohim's love was no longer just an "abstract concept", a show of compassion from a distance. As Jesus Messiah Christ, **Elohim** went the full distance showing His Love to the world even as most of it still hated Him for even coming. He shed his sinless/human blood to "forgive us all our sins" and "redeem" us from our sins. Jesus the God-man Messiah, took our sins in His own body so we wouldn't have to suffer the eternal

---

[69] Hebrews 2:17-18 (NIV)

[70] Hebrews 4:15 (NIV)

[71] Hebrews 1:3 (NIV)

[72] Colossians 1:15 (The Message Bible)

[73] John 13:1 (NIV)

consequences of our own sinful failures. It is written, *"God demonstrates His own love for us in this; While we were still sinners, Christ died for us."* [74] For it is written, *"You were dead in sins, and your sinful desires were not yet cut away. Then He {Elohim} gave you a share in the very life of Christ, for He forgave all your sins, and blotted out the charges proved against you, the list of His commandments which you had not obeyed. He took this list of sins and destroyed it by nailing it to Christ's cross. In this way God took away Satan's power to accuse you of sin, and God openly displayed to the whole world Christ's triumph at the cross where your sins were all taken away."* [75]

How far did *Elohim* go to show us His unfathomable Love for humankind? Jesus Christ took on ALL the sin from Adam to the end of time, as if He, Himself, in our place, had committed them all, so that we might know, not only what sinless freedom is like, but that you and I would come to know what real LOVE looks like. The innocent for the guilty, taking the full penalty of all our wrongs upon Himself in order to set us free from them, and tie us back in relationship with our Creator in righteous standing; no longer separated from our Creator Father. That, my friends, is a pure BODY OF LOVE

No wonder the writer of Hebrews declares, *"the blood of Christ, who through the eternal Spirit offered Himself unblemished to God, cleanse our consciences from acts that lead to death."* [76] Paul writes a few verses later, *"so Christ was*

---

[74] Romans 5:8 (NIV)

[75] CoLossians 2:13-15 (Living Bible)

[76] Hebrews 9:14 (NIV)

sacrificed once to take away the sins of many people." [77] And again, it is written, *"God made (Jesus) who had no sin to be sin (or be a sin offering) for us, so that in (Jesus) we might become the righteousness of God."* [78] This is why it is written, *"For if, when we were God's enemies, we were reconciled to Him through the death of His Son, how much more, having been reconciled, shall we be saved through His life!"* (How much more? Much, much more. Guaranteed!) [79] The disciple Peter describes this purpose in profound terms, *"Christ also suffered. He died once for the sins of all us guilty sinners although he himself was innocent of any sin at any time, that he might bring us safely home to God."* [80]

Elohim came in a Body to take back the dominion of Earth for mankind. He also used that same Body to restore mankind to his original state by making believers sinless again through the sacrifice of His prepared body's sinless blood. For it is written this way, *"For God was pleased to have all his fullness dwell in Him, and through Him to reconcile to Himself all things, whether things on earth or things in heaven, by making peace through His blood, shed on the cross. Once you were alienated from God and were enemies in your minds because of your evil behavior. But now He has reconciled you by Christ's "physical body" through death, to present you holy in His sight, without blemish and free from accusation."* [81] And in another place it

---

[77] Hebrews 9:28 (NIV)

[78] 2 Corinthians 5:21 (NIV)

[79] Romans 5:8,10 (NIV)

[80] 1 Peter 3:18 (Living Bible)

[81] Colossians 1:19 –22 (NIV)

is written, *"And by that will, we have been made holy through the sacrifice of the body of Christ once for all."* [82] And again it is written, *"For by that one offering He has made forever perfect in the sight of God all those whom He is making holy."* [83]

And finally, *"This is how we know what love is: Jesus Christ laid down His life for us."* [84] Why? Because: LOVE MUST HAVE A BODY.

---

[82] Hebrews 10:10 (NIV)

[83] Hebrews 10:14 (Living Bible)

[84] 1 John 3:16 (NIV)

CHAPTER TWELVE

Why Unconditional Love

M any argue that "all roads lead to God," regardless of the beliefs. However, there is only one Faith that presents a Loving Father who expresses "unconditional" love. Mankind in its sinful state would never devise such a faith that presents "unconditional love" and "acceptance" at its core. It is a foreign notion to all other world religions, and to our entrenched psyche that we could somehow be granted "complete and permanent immunity" against inevitable consequences or punishment for things we have done wrong in our lives. There is always some kind of "penance' or 'performance" attached to all other beliefs so that mankind can "make up" for wrongs done. The act of total and complete "acquittal", without the "penalty" for injustice, is outside the scope of our human experience.

Man-made religions ideologies will always have at their core the condition that mankind must continually "*do something*" to "*get something*". No other belief outside pure Christianity offers "Grace without works." All religions require humans qualify themselves by doing something to get something. This is how we know Christ is of God and the ONLY way to **Elohim**; because the work has *already been done*, the price paid for mankind's sin. It is impossible for mankind to save itself, because we cannot change our behavior absent a divine encounter. The act of **Elohim's** pure Love made it possible, for you and I to come to God without fear of condemnation, or judgment of any kind. You only have to believe He forgives and accepts you to get *divine* Grace's benefits. There's no cost to you, no premium to pay, no self-mutilation or debt, no penance to do, no obstacles to overcome, no performance to qualify. All requirements were accomplished through Christ Jesus' *body* and sacrifice of Love for you and me. There can be no greater LOVE than this: Love *"appeared" in a body.* [85] Why? Because LOVE MUST HAVE A BODY.

You see, the law of sin and guilt makes men "hide" from God just as Adam and Eve hide when they sinned. The law of "Grace" allows mankind to safely come into God's presence without fear of judgment or reprisal. If there weren't "unconditional" acceptance (which is Grace) to come before God, no one would do it willingly. But through the sacrifice of Jesus' *body*, Grace ushers us into His presence "uncondemned" so we can, without fear, repent and find *forgiveness* and remove the eternal consequences of the *"guilt of sin."* [86] For it is written, *"This is how God showed his love among us. He sent His one and only {begotten Son] into the world that we might live through Him. This is love: not that we loved God, but that He loved us and sent His Son as an atoning sacrifice for [taking away] our sins."* [87] In another place it is written, *"But God put his love on the line for us by offering his Son in sacrificial death while we were of no use whatever to him."* [88]

Grace was God's gift to humankind, by and through the "body" of Christ Jesus. Why? *"Because of His great love for us, God, who is rich in mercy, made us alive with Christ even when we were dead in transgressions; it is by grace you have been*

---

[85] I Timothy 3:16 (NIV)

[86] Romans 6:7 (NIV)

[87] 1 John 4:9-10 (NIV)

[88] Romans 5:8 (The Message Bible)

saved. *And God raised us up with Christ and seated us with Him in the heavenly realms in Christ Jesus, in order that in the coming ages He might show the incomparable riches of His grace, expressed in His kindness to us in Christ Jesus."* [89]

God really wants you to know how much He loves you. Through His Holy Spirit living in us when He saves us, you and I now share a love far beyond our ability to understand it. This opportunity stems directly from demonstrating His love in the body of Christ Jesus to redeem us from the consequences of our sins. For it is written, *"He himself bore our sins in his body on the tree, so that we might die to sins and live for righteousness; by his wounds you have been healed."* [90] Now we can know what real love looks like. Paul offers this prayer for all believers, *"May your roots go down deep into the soil of God's marvelous love; and may you be able to feel and understand, as all God's children should, how long, how wide, how deep, and how high His love really is; and to experience this love for yourselves, though it is so great that you will never see the end of it or fully know or understand it."* [91]

---

[89] Ephesians 2:3-8 (Living Bible)
[90] I Peter 2:24 (NIV)
[91] Ephesians 3:18-19 (Living Bible)

CHAPTER THIRTEEN

Why Grace

I t is important to understand Why Grace is central to our Salvation. As we have already discovered: without Grace *(unconditional acceptance)* we could never approach God with any confidence. Why? Because we would be too afraid a Holy God would hurt us, rather than help us. This is why, if we are to "grow in Grace", it cannot be from a place of fear of condemnation. This is why it is written, *"There is therefore, no condemnation to those who are in Christ Jesus."* [92] Of course, this does not mean there isn't "instruction" or "training". And it doesn't mean there aren't consequences in our lives for deliberate disobedience against the instruction and training Holy Spirit provides.

Our status however, has been forever changed by Grace. We are not just "saved people", we have been made "sons and daughters" with all rights of righteous inheritance through Christ Jesus. That inheritance includes "imputed" righteousness. For it is written: *"How great is the love the Father has lavished on us, that we should be called children of God! And that is what we are!"* [93] And again it is written, *"since we have confidence to enter the Most Holy Place by the blood of Jesus, by a new and living way opened for us through the curtain, that is, his body, and since we have a great priest over the house of God, let us draw near to God with a sincere heart in full assurance of faith, having our hearts sprinkled to cleanse us from a guilty conscience."* [94]

Grace allows me the opportunity to get right today, what

[92] Romans 8:1 (NIV)

[93] 1 John 3:1 (NIV)

[94] Hebrews 10 17-22 (Jerusalem Bible)

I failed to get right the day before. It is written, *"Because of his kindness, you have been saved through trusting Christ. And even trusting is not of yourselves; it too is a gift from God. Salvation is not a reward for the good we have done, so none of us can take any credit for it."* [95] The scriptures, however, also tell us to live in a manner that reflects our new found position of Grace in Christ.

Grace expects an *active response*, not just *passive acceptance*. We must learn to emulate, in visible ways, our gratitude for the Grace our heavenly Father has lavished on us. In essence, our lives should reflect a proper "Thank You" to Grace. For it is written, *"we pray this in order that you may live a life worthy of the Lord and may please Him in every way, bearing fruit in every good work, growing in the knowledge of God."* [96] Because of His unconditional Grace toward us, everything we do and say must be a "Thank You" to Grace. Grace is never a good excuse for bad behavior. Grace was never meant to be a license (or cover) for deliberate disobedience or continued lawless behavior.

The idea of Grace is this: that God's character would ultimately be reflected in every aspect of one's life to the same extent that there would be no distinction between the actions of the man or woman, and the actions of his/her God. We are to be a *"Work Of Grace"*, not just an *"Object of Grace"*. Grace is granted to us so *"that we might be for the "Praise of His glory."* [97] Grace doesn't make God turn a blind eye to sinful behavior; it

---

[95] Ephesians 2:8-9 (Living Bible)

[96] Colossians 1:10 (NIV)

[97] Ephesian 1:12 (NIV)

merely allows us another opportunity to change that behavior. Thank God His *"mercies are new every morning"*. [98] God would not call us to something greater if He had already placed us there. For we all are called to *"press on toward the goal to win the prize for which God has called {us} heavenward in Christ Jesus."* [99]

Grace is meant to cover us while we actively pursue a greater excellence in our conduct and character which mirrors more and more the "ultimate" godly image; which is (Christ Jesus). It is written, *"Just as you used to offer the parts of your body in slavery to impurity and to ever-increasing wickedness, so now offer them in slavery to righteousness leading to holiness. (righteousness for your sanctification) or, (for the purposes of becoming truly good)."* [100] We occupy the position of "righteousness" while we are being *conformed* and *transformed* into His "holiness". Paul writes to the Colossians, *"you have taken off your old self with its practices and have put on the new self, which is being renewed in knowledge in the image of its Creator."* [101]

The disciple Peter instructs believers to add to their faith a number of spiritual divine character qualities in their pursuit of excellence and transformation, as evidence that Grace is having its intended effect. He writes, *"For this very reason, make every effort to add to your faith, goodness; and to goodness, knowledge; and to knowledge, self-control; and to self-control, perseverance;*

---

[98] Colossians 3:9-10 (NIV)
[99] Philippians 3:14 (NIV)
[100] Romans 6:19 (NIV)
[101] 2 Peter 1:5-8 (NIV)

and to perseverance, godliness; and to godliness, brotherly kindness; and to brotherly kindness, love. For if you possess these qualities in increasing measure, they will keep you from being ineffective and unproductive in your knowledge of our Lord Jesus Christ." [102] The written Word encourages us in that, as long as we are actively pursuing these godly characteristics, we need not worry to fail in achieving this objective. It is written, *"run in such a way as to get the prize."* [103] The Message Bible reflects the desire we all should strive to emulate, *"I'm off and running, and I'm not turning back."*

I have often said: *"What you do has eternal value only in respect to what you become".* It's not in the "doing" so much as it is in the "becoming". When you "become" what the Word says, *everything you do* has eternal value. If you only "do" without "becoming", nothing you "do" has eternal value.

---

[102] 2 Peter 1:5-8 (NIV)

[103] 1 Corinthians 9:24 (Living Bible)

CHAPTER FOURTEEN

Why Christ Left Believers "Unfinished" Business

Jesus Christ, the God-man in a human Body, bought back mankind's domain and authority by His own blood at the cross. Christ handed Earth back to His believers to rule and reign over. He gave His believers the authority to rule over all principalities and powers of the air. Christ Jesus expects His believers to do something with that authority. In fact, He commands it. Christ's commands are clear, *Go! "love your neighbor as yourself" and "anyone who has faith in me will do what I have been doing. He will do even greater things than these, because I am going to the Father."* [104] Why? Because this is our world, our place of authority. We are commissioned to complete that which remains unfinished and, to present our results back to our Lord and Savior at the appointed time.

Of course, this raises the obvious question; What were the works of Messiah? And, how are we to accomplish what He left unfinished for us to finish? How do We accomplish this? We do it the way Jesus Christ did it. What is His example? We, *"Follow the way of (agape Love.)"*. [105] Love is the defining mark of God's relationship with mankind. It is the mark by which the world will know we are children of God. Without the "expression" of God-like Love, we cannot say we know or are even known by God. For it is written, *"And this is His command: to believe in the name of His Son, Jesus Christ, and to love one another as He commanded us. Those who obey His commands live in Him, and He in them."* [106]

---

[104] John 14:12 (NIV)

[105] I Corinthians 14:1 (NIV)

[106] 1 John 3:23-24 (NIV)

Love is an "action" word, not just a feeling toward someone. Without action there is no "expression" and without expression, there is no "confirmation" that love actually exists. God showed His love by "action". *"Love one another. As I have loved you, so you must love one another. By this, everyone will know that you are my disciples, if you love one another."* [107] In other words, *"let's stop just saying we love people let us really love them, and show it by our actions."* [108]

This can be expressed in many ways big and small. Love is love, regardless of the size of the deed or word spoken. A smile, a word of encouragement, a prayer, changing someone's car tire beside the road, a helping hand, offering food to the hungry, introducing people to their heavenly Father for reconciliation and salvation. In fact Jesus Christ made it as simple as it gets, *"If you give a cup of water in my name, (Jesus) there is a reward."* In fact, God's Word tells us, *"whatever you do, whether in word or deed, do it all in the name of the Lord Jesus, giving thanks to God the Father through him."* [109]

As individuals, or as a collective, our purpose as believers is to show how "good" God is and to reflect that goodness in all its various forms. *"The time has come,"* Jesus said, *"The kingdom of God is near. Repent and believe the good news!"* [110] The message of Jesus is indeed "good news"; the promise of life over death,

---

[107] John 13:34-35 (NIV)

[108] 1 John 3:18 (Living Bible)

[109] Colossians 3:17 (NIV)

[110] Mark 1:15 (NIV)

the promise of peace over conflict, the promise of abundant life over lack, healing over disease, eternal life over death.

Jesus said it this way, *"If you, then, though you are evil, know how to give good gifts to your children, how much more will your Father in heaven give good gifts to those who ask Him!"* [111] If God gives rain to the just and unjust, there can be no doubt that HE will give good gifts to those who seek Him wholeheartedly. And as God is our Teacher, He urges us to reflect His divine "character" by doing good to others as the opportunity presents itself. For it is written, *"A good man brings good things out of the good stored up in him."* [112] And, it is to that end we live in such a way that when the time comes, our Lord and Savior and Redeemer will utter the two greatest words our ears will ever hear; *"Well done" good and faithful servant. You have been faithful with a few things; I will put you in charge of many things. Come and share your master's happiness."* [113]

It is interesting to note that the very first thing the disciple Peter instructs believers to add to their faith is "virtue" (or goodness). The outcome of our expression of love is left up to God. But every good deed, kind word, expression of divine love shown, reflects what Jesus Christ came to Earth to demonstrate up close and personal. As true believers, we must show *"proof that our deeds are as good as our beliefs."* But, we don't do good just to get a reward, we do good to be like our heavenly Father **Elohim**. It is written, *"For we are God's workmanship, created*

---

[111] Matthew 7:11 (NIV)

[112] Matthew 12:35 (NIV)

[113] Matthew 25:21 (NIV)

in Christ Jesus to do good works, which God prepared in advance for us to do." [114] By becoming like our Father ***Elohim*** in love, everything good we do reflects and affirms the "becoming" part of our transformation process. *"let your light shine before others, that they may see **your good deeds** and glorify your Father in heaven."* [115]

Says **Benedictine Monk David Steindl-Rast** *"the fruit is an increase in love, patience and compassion for others, leaving behind the unmistakable taste of holiness."*

And so it is written, *"live a life of love, just as Christ loved us and gave himself up for us as a fragrant offering and sacrifice to God."* [116]

---

[114] Ephesians 2:10 (NIV)

[115] Matthew 5:16 (NIV)

[116] Ephesians 5:2 (NIV)

CHAPTER FIFTEEN

Why God Commands Us to Love

You can command obedience but you cannot, in a human sense, command love. So why did Christ command us to love? Because HE could give no other. *Elohim* Is Love, and if *"God has poured out His love into our hearts by the Holy Spirit, whom He has given us,"* [117] we can reflect no less the fulfillment of that command than to Love. This is why it is written, *"We know that we have passed from death to life, because we love our brothers."* [118] If we love one another, we too, will show it by our actions. God gives us the ability to love as He loves. In fact, it is the act of showing *Love* that is the essence of Faith, reflected through us in our actions. For it is written, *"For in Him (Jesus) the only thing that counts is Faith, expressing itself through love."* [119] And again it is written, *"it isn't enough just to say you have faith. You must also do good to prove that you have it. Faith that doesn't show itself by good works is no faith at all."*[120]

So, how is love actually demonstrated? And how will the world know what love looks like so that it's not confused with basic human sympathy or compassion for the needs of others? We know Jesus Christ gave us the directive, *"A new command I give you; Love one another, as I have loved you, so you must love one another. By this everyone will know that you are my disciples, if you love one another."* [121] But the love expressed to the world has to be more than just good deeds. It has to embody

---

[117] Romans 5:5 (NIV)

[118] 1 John 3:14 (NIV)

[119] Galatians 5:6 (NIV)

[120] James 2:17 (Living Bible)

[121] John 13: 34-35 (NIV)

the *Character* and *Spirit* of Jesus that connects with the very soul and spirit of the people our lives encounter, in order to introduce them to *divine* life. It is one of the top two commands of **Elohim**. *"Love the Lord your God with all your heart and with all your soul and with all your mind."* It is the golden rule in everything: *"Love your neighbor as yourself."*[122]

This command does not require reciprocation of any kind by the receiving party. It is written, *"And this is love: that we walk in obedience to His commands. As you have heard from the beginning, His command is that you walk in love."* [123] It is to be done absent any and all expectations of any kind. They might appreciate what you say or do and they might not. But their response is not at issue, God's *love* is. Their conduct or behavior have no bearing on the command to treat others as you would like to be treated. Do you want grace to come to you when you don't deserve it? Then give it to someone else who doesn't deserve it.

This difference separates worldly compassion from divine order. **Elohim**'s love is not concerned with getting something in return such as thanks, appreciation or applause. God shows His love to a disbelieving world every day by giving them sunshine, rain and food whether they acknowledge Him or not. We are directed to emulate this divine quality, by loving people as God loves them in the anticipation that men and women will acknowledge their need for God's love.

The command is simple enough, *"since God so loved us, we*

---

[122] Matthew 22: 37,39 (NIV)

[123] 2 John 1:6 (NIV)

also ought to love one another." [124] Paul's letter to the Romans sums it up this way, *"Let no debt remain outstanding, except the continuing debt to love one another, for he who loves his fellow man has fulfilled the law. Love does no harm to its neighbor. Therefore love is the fulfillment of the law."* [125]

---

[124] 1 John 4:11 (NIV)
[125] Romans 13:8,10 (NIV)

CHAPTER SIXTEEN

Why There is a Body of Believers with Greater Things to Do

When Christ Jesus hung on the cross, His dying words were, *"it is finished"*. [126] So what did Christ mean when he states, *"anyone who has faith in me will do what I have been doing. He will do even greater things than these, because I am going to the Father."* [127] What, if anything, did Jesus Christ leave unfinished? What does Christ consider as greater things than what He did while on earth in a body? What does that look like? And, how are we to accomplish these greater things than what Christ did?

When Messiah Christ was here, He did countless miracles. In fact the Book of John closes with the statement that if everything Christ said and did were written down, he felt the world could not contain the books that could be written about them. However, Jesus was one man in one place at a single time in history. With the Body of Believers and, through the Holy Spirit, Christ Jesus can be everywhere at once in physical form through His believing children. It is written, *"if you give yourself to the Lord, you and Christ are joined together as one."* [128] In this way the Body of Believers can do "greater things" than Messiah Christ did as one man.

It is our turn to show Love in its "purest form" to the world in ever increasing measure as a mirror image of our Lord and Savior Christ Jesus. It is written in this way, *"All these new things are from God who brought us back to himself through what Christ Jesus did. And God has given us the privilege of*

---

[126] John 19:30 (NIV)

[127] John 14:12 (NIV)

[128] 1 Corinthians 6:17 (Living Bible)

urging everyone to come into his favor and be reconciled to him. For God was in Christ, restoring the world to himself, no longer counting men's sins against them but blotting them out. This is the wonderful message he has given us to tell others." [129]

So, what does reconciliation look like? It is written, *"Do not cause anyone to stumble, whether Jews, Greeks or the church of God, even as I try to please everybody in every way. For I am not seeking my own good but the good of many, so that they may be saved."* [130] Just as Jesus Christ set aside His garments and humbled Himself to wash His disciples feet as an act of love and reconciliation of mankind, not counting men's sins against them, so we, standing in Christ's stead, are called to mirror that same humility in reconciling others to Christ in love. For it is written, *"Live such good lives among the pagans* (unbelievers) *that, though they accuse you of doing wrong, they may see your good deeds and glorify God on the day he visits us."* [131]

---

[129] 2 Corinthians 5:18-19 (Living Bible)

[130] I Corinthians 10:32-33 (NIV)

[131] I Peter 2:12 (NIV)

CHAPTER SEVENTEEN

Why Love Uses Touch

There is nothing more healing than the power of touch. Even science recognizes this fact. The brush of a mother's hand across the fevered brow of her child. A soft tender caress and the warmth of the arms that hold tightly. Science can't explain it, but it recognizes that "touch" has a healing quality to it. Christ Jesus was always reaching out to touch someone in healing. *"Little children were brought to Jesus for him to place his hands on them and pray for them."* [132] There is something about the Holy Spirit within us that is transmitted through touch in ministry to others. It is written, *"let us love one another, (or practice loving each other) for love comes from God. "Everyone who loves has been born of God and knows God. No one has ever seen God; but if we love one another, God lives in us and His love is made complete in us."* [133]

Now if Love is made complete in us, our touch, empowered by Holy Spirit carries life and healing to others. When we use touch, the eternal life within us flows out and healing results. It is written, *"If the Spirit of him who raised Jesus from the dead is living in you, He who raised Christ from the dead will also give life to your mortal bodies through His Spirit, who lives in you."* [134] Paul prays similarly for the Ephesians that they might understand just how great a power resides in them; *"I pray also that the eyes of your heart may be enlightened in order that you may know the hope to which he has called you, the riches of his glorious inheritance in the saints, and his incomparably great*

---

[132] Matthew 19:13 (NIV)

[133] I John 4:7,12 (NIV)

[134] Romans 8:11 (NIV)

power for us who believe. That power is like the working of His mighty strength, which He exerted in Christ when He raised Him from the dead." [135]

It is now your turn to demonstrate to others, the power of *divine touch* as *Christ*-ians or, (little Christs'). As born again Believers, we are the body of Christ to the world.

---

[135] Ephesians 1:18-20 (NIV)

CHAPTER EIGHTEEN

Why Believers Celebrate the Passover Communion

When we, as a believers, celebrate the Passive meal, our minds immediately are drawn to Jesus' words as He spoke to the people, *"I am the living bread that came down from heaven. If anyone eats of this bread, he will live forever. Jesus* continues; *unless you eat the flesh of the Son of Man and drink his blood, you have no life in you."* [136] Then our thoughts turn to the last night Jesus would spend with his disciple before facing the redemptive cross. *"After taking the cup, he gave thanks and said, "Take this and divide it among you. This cup is the new covenant in my blood, which is poured out for you.* And he took bread, gave thanks and broke it, and gave it to them, saying, *"This is my body given for you; do this in remembrance of me."* [137]

Tradition has taught us, when taking the bread and the cup, to focus primarily on our *unilateral* relationship to Christ; seeing only Jesus and oneself and what the ceremony means to us personally. Might this reverent ceremony hold a much deeper meaning and purpose? Do the elements, which symbolizing the "Body and Blood" of Christ, hold a far deeper spiritual dimension than just Christ and me alone in communion?

In pondering this question over the years what broader, deeper meaning the Passover meal may hold, my mind and imagination has often been drawn to the legendary Three Musketeers or even King Arthur's knights of the Round Table. Realizing the "round table" signifies an unbroken chain or Oneness, my visual image focuses on a group of men as they finish their meal together. They have eaten and drank as

---

[136] John 5:51-54 (NIV)

[137] Luke 22: 17-22 (NIV)

ONE MAN, expressed in their mantra code which binds them together as ONE. I picture them as they stand, cups raised in unison as if ONE inter-connected inter-locking being, echoing as if only ONE Voice, their enduring words ringing in my consciousness; *"All for ONE and ONE For All."*

In contemplating this visual image, my thoughts immediately turn to the apostle Paul's writings to the Church at Corinth and the deeper meaning the Passover ceremony may hold in his consciousness. Paul reflects this deeper understanding of the Passover meal when he writes. *"For Christ's love compels us, because we are convinced that **one died for all**, and therefore all died. And **he died for all, that those who live should** no longer live for themselves but **for "him" who died for them** and was raised again."* [138]

COMMUNION or PASSOVER, as some prefer to call it, is not merely bread and cup to reflect merely a "vertical" ceremonial relationship between you and Christ alone, it is a spiritual remembrance of the *ONENESS* we all share in Christ Jesus. Jesus' final prayer, before offering himself to the extreme torture and agony of the cross, is significant to understanding the *Common-union* or Passover ceremony. What was Christ' last prayer? It was for our ONENESS.

"For I'm no longer going to be visible in the world; They'll continue in the world While I return to you.
Holy Father, guard them as they pursue this life That you conferred as a gift through me,

---

[138] 2 Corinthians 5:14-15 (NIV)

So they can be one heart and mind As we are one heart and mind."

"Make them holy—consecrated—with the truth;
In the same way that you gave me a mission in the world,
I give them a mission in the world.
I'm consecrating myself for their sakes
So they'll be truth-consecrated in their mission."
"The goal is for all of them to become one heart and mind—
Just as you, Father, are in me and I in you,
So they might be one heart and mind with us.
Then the world might believe that you, in fact, sent me.
The same glory you gave me, I gave them,
So they'll be as unified and together as we are—
I in them and you in me.
Then they'll be mature in this oneness,
And give the godless world evidence
That you've sent me and loved them
In the same way you've loved me." [139]

In reality, Christ handed His disciples just ONE cup, which they all drank from, symbolizing the *ONENESS* He desired them to live in. Paul often refers to this as being only ONE cup. He writes to the Corinthians, *"Careless communion means spiritual weakness; let us take due care. It is this careless participation which is the reason for the many feeble and sickly Christians in your church and the explanation of the fact that*

---

[139] John 17: 10-12, 18-19, 21-23 (The Message Bible)

many of you are spiritually asleep." [140] The Corinthians failed to properly understand the purpose of the Passover communion-celebration. His Body is US, and when we don't see US as a ONE with one common purpose under the same Lord and Savior, we miss the very essence of the Communion (or, common-union) celebration. It celebrates that the **ONE for ALL** (Jesus-the Christ) was for the-Body of Believers as we **ALL live FOR THE ONE** (Christ Jesus).

It is Christ's ultimate prayer that WE, as Believers, be ONE. It is written, "*The body is a unit, though it is made up of many parts; and though all its parts are many, they form one body. So it is with Christ.*" [141] It is this "Community of ONE," that this celebration was given to US as One Body of Believers. For it is written, "*Is not the cup of thanksgiving for which we give thanks a participation in the blood of Christ? And is not the bread that we break a participation in the body of Christ? Because there is "one" loaf, we, who are many, are "one" body, for we all partake of the "one" loaf.*" [142]

Therefore, communion is recognizing the right relationship of the community of believers with which we fellowship. Paul writes to the Ephesians encouraging them and us to come into Unity. He writes: "*I pray that out of His glorious riches He (Christ) may strengthen you with power through His Spirit in your inner being, so that Christ may dwell in your hearts through faith. And I pray that you, being rooted and established in love,*

---

[140] I Corinthians 11:31(J.B. Phillips Translation)

[141] I Corinthians 12:12 (NIV)

[142] I Corinthians 10:16-17 (NIV)

may have power, together with all the saints, to grasp how wide and long and high and deep is the love of Christ, and to know this love that surpasses knowledge – that you may be filled to the measure of all the fullness of God. Now to Him who is able to do immeasurably more than all we ask or imagine, according to His power that is at work within us." [143] It is the supreme Calling.

It is the ONE Spirit by which WE are all baptized into as ONE body, ONE family. Collectively, WE are **all for One** and **One for all** in Christ Jesus. Paul expresses this idea to the Thessalonians when he writes: *"Your faith has made such strides, and **your love, each for all and all for each**, ..."* [144]

So the next time you lift the bread and cup of Passover (or, *common-union*) celebration, visualize Christ Jesus at the head of the table and you, along with your fellow brothers and sisters in Christ, all lifting a cup as if ONE cup, ONE body; and saying to your Lord and Savior: you were the *ONE for All,* and we are now the *All for the ONE.*

---

[143] Ephesians 3:16-20 (NIV)
[144] Thessalonians 1:3 (J. B. Phillips Translation)

CHAPTER NINETEEN

Why You Are Here

We are to "mirror" to others what Christ Jesus did for us, otherwise, the world won't know God loves them. Satan's way is to remind people just how bad they are and that they are worthless or unredeemable. He is the *"accuser of all God's children"*. [145] He doesn't want people to know that they can "boldly" and freely come to God, without reservation or fear of condemnation, to confess and repent without fear of reprisal or judgment to the One who loves them unconditionally. It is written, *"if we confess our sins, He is faithful and just to forgive us all our sins."* [146] Why? Jesus continues to be a mediator of the New Covenant on our behalf; which gives us "continued access" to deal with our mistakes and shortcomings, and the opportunity to do it "right" the next time without fear of condemnation.

You are alive for a reason and purpose. This is why the scriptures tell us to practice, practice and more practice to "do" good, because to be good is to do good. You can't just be good; Good must be demonstrated in order to be seen as good. The Living Bible puts it this way; *"God is not unjust; He will not forget your work and the love you have shown Him as you have helped His people and continue to help them. And we are anxious that you keep right on loving others as long as life lasts, so that you will get your full reward."* [147] Notice the text when it says God will not forget, *"the love you have shown HIM."* Who? Christ Jesus. How? by helping His people. I am reminded of Christ

---

[145] Revelation 12:10 (NIV)

[146] I John 1:9 (NIV)

[147] Hebrews 6:10-11 (NIV)

Jesus' words when He said, *"whatever you did for one of the least of these brothers (and sisters) of mine, you did for me."* [148]

Therefore, as we have opportunity, let us do good to all people." [149]

---

[148] Matthew 25:40 (NIV)
[149] Galatians 6:10 (NIV)

CHAPTER TWENTY

Why Wait Any Longer

W hy wait any longer to experience the Love of Jesus Christ in its fullness? HIS love is so great that it goes beyond our understanding or ability to fathom it in human terms. *Elohim* loves you soooo much that He showed it "up close and personal", by coming in the likeness of a human man, to touch you, hold you, heal you and redeem you back to Himself. Why? So you and I could know what perfect and pure *Love* looks like, the kind that transcends our ability to define it. It cannot be defined, it can only be experienced and then reflected back.

It's your turn to both experience Love and, in turn, reflect Love. LOVE MUST HAVE A BODY, so what are you waiting for?

A Prayer Of Invitation

Heavenly Father, I want to know your love completely
I've lived much of my life filled with distractions
That have taken me away from knowing you and your love
Forgive me for all these wrongs
I renounce everything in my life that is not of you
I'm reaching out to Christ Jesus, who has
so wondrously reached out for me
I want to lay hold on those things, which bring
Into my life, your presence in abundance
I begin anew to live my life in a way to become
all that Christ Jesus has saved me for and wants me to be
I'm off and running, and I'm not turning back
I'm forgetting the past and looking forward to what lies ahead
With arms outstretched, I reach for my goal
to receive the prize of honoring my Lord and savior

because of what Christ Jesus has done for me
In the Name above every Name, Christ Jesus my Lord

A Prayer of Blessings
I pray that your hearts will be flooded with light
so that you can see something of the
future he has called you to share.
I pray that you will begin to understand how incredibly great
his power is to help those who believe him.
May the Lord continually bless you with heaven's blessings
as well as with human joys.
May your roots go down deep into the
soil of God's marvelous love;
and may you be able to feel and understand, as
all God's children should, how long, how wide,
how deep, and how high His love really is;
and to experience this love for yourselves.
Though it is so great that you will never see the end of it
or fully know or understand it."
May every fiber of your being unite in reverence
to His glorious name.
Amen!

In the coming months, Look for the new exciting Series by T. L. Harper entitled:

The New Kingdom Order Series

Upcoming Titles include:
The Two Sides Of Grace
The Companions of Faith,
The Art Of Obedience,
A Question Of Gifts Inheritance and Reward,
The Fellowship of the Cup,

And other great Titles that will change the way you see and live Christianity. These works will, for many, alter the very foundation on which your faith and service exists. You will become alive in Christ with new determination to become all that Christ intends.

T L Harper Welcomes Reader Feedback
Send your thoughts and comments to:
lovemusthaveabody@gmail.com